D0261719

To my sister, Maria – S.K.

For my cousin, Keith Newson – T.T.

First published in Great Britain in 2008 by Bloomsbury Publishing Plc
36 Soho Square, London, W1D 3QY

Text copyright © Tracey Turner 2008
Illustrations copyright © Sally Kindberg 2008

The moral rights of the author and illustrator have been asserted

A CIP catalogue record of this book is available from the British Library

ISBN 978 0 7475 9431 4

All papers used by Bloomsbury Publishing are natural, recyclable products made from wood grown
in well-managed forests. The manufacturing processes conform to the environmental regulations
of the country of origin.

Printed in Singapore

1 3 5 7 9 10 8 6 4 2

www.bloomsbury.com

the COMIC STRIP

ooh!

History
of the
World

nng

Sally Kindberg
and Tracey Turner

BLOOMSBURY
CHILDREN'S
BOOKS

Contents

HOW IT ALL STARTED (PROBABLY)

They were **WILD** and they were **HAIRY** – Yes it was **EARLY MAN**

About 3 million years ago, human-like creatures evolved...

And about time too...

ugh?

PLIP PLOP

Could someone please hurry up and discover **FIRE**?

brrr

brr!

stop it!

By around one and a half million years ago...

Yum! Now we won't get poisoned by raw meat! (...much)

STONE AGE

TOOL KIT

big stone

medium sized stone

very small stone

small stone

er... stick

About 100,000 years ago, our ancestors appeared in AFRICA. The other types of humans gradually died out...

(Well, most of them did)

The new HUMANS didn't stay in one place...

and so...

3

CIVILISATION IS BORN!

Meanwhile, other civilisations were now popping up all over the place...

The ancient Egyptians had lots of strange gods...

and habits...

Rich ancient Egyptians had their dead bodies made into MUMMIES.

mmm

Squelchy bits taken out and soaked for 40 days →

brain

TUG
TUG

dried squelchy bits put into Canopic jars...

empty body was plumped out with sawdust and rags

then...

and...

fancy mask

nice

pet

snacks for afterlife

Meanwhile, over in ...

And further south...

the Indus Valley

civilisation had existed for hundreds of years. But we don't know much about it due to the...

No one knows why they disappeared.
Unlike another ancient civilisation...

ANCIENT GREECE

Invaders from the North arrived

DELPHI

THEBES
ATHENS

SICYON

CORINTH
MYCENAE

ARG°S

OLYMPIA

SPARTA

They built separate city-states all over Greece

Those Spartans are a funny lot!

Have you seen the state of those Olympian beards?

Never trust an Athenian, I say.

Hurrah!

The biggest city-state was ATHENS. Some states were ruled by kings but ATHENS was a DEMOCRACY.

And we shall all be equal and vote in political elections!

Hurrah

Yes, hurrah!

Er, not you women actually

That's a bit unfair, isn't it?

Tut!

What!!

Boo!

...and not slaves, obviously.

But while Greece was divided...
the huge PERSIAN empire attacked

The war with the Persians went
on for decades. Until finally...

...the united Greeks won

This left time for other things, such as THINKING

... and DRAMA

(Some of it was – ahem – rather rude!)

But peace between states didn't last long. ATHENS and SPARTA went to war...

It wasn't long before another army arrived in Greece...

Meanwhile, another lot of
conquering was going on...

And there was more fighting until Rome got its first EMPEROR...

THE FALL OF THE ROMAN EMPIRE

Hello... I'm Augustus Caesar, EMPEROR of Rome

All this is mine... all mine

CACKLE

Emperors came and went...

CALIGULA dressed as a goddess and made his horse a politician.

GLUG

Steady on!

He drank pearls dissolved in vinegar and generally was a mad, evil tyrant.

CLAUDIUS made a law allowing people to fart at dinner.

He died after he was fed poisoned mushrooms by his wife.

hnng!!

KILL!!

KILL!

KILL!!

froth froth

I think he's in one of his moods

NERO sentenced his first wife to death, killed his second wife and had his own mother murdered.

heh heh

COMMODUS fought as a gladiator. He always won because his opponents' weapons were made of lead.

25

At about the same time, over in the PACIFIC...

the POLYNESIANS

The POLYNESIANS lived on islands
scattered about in the Pacific Ocean

And now it was about time for...

The Dark Ages

Elsewhere...

In the GUPTA empire in Northern India, brilliant mathematicians, astronomers and philosophers were at work

...and the number 0

We invented the decimal system!

But...

the pesky Huns destroyed us in 500.

sums →

← more sums

Bother!

The MAYAN civilisation was the most powerful in the Americas

We have a written language

and lovely calendars like this

...and the odd bit of human sacrifice never hurt anyone.

heh heh

...and over in

Ch'ang-an, the capital of the TANG dynasty, was the biggest city in the world

Female Tang ruler Wu Zetian was the only Empress in Chinese history.

Definitely

Our silk and porcelain are the best

I'm the boss OK!

By about 850 the huge ISLAMIC empire included Spain, North Africa, Persia and Syria.

Our empire's bigger than the Roman Empire...

And we know loads about science...

Massive!!

But we don't like to brag...

much

Further north there was a lot of pillaging going on...

And in the East it paid to be fierce too
(some were better at it than others)

Meanwhile, empires grew in other parts of the world...

41

And by the 14th century, a different kind of fever was sweeping Europe...

But not everyone was dying of plague...

There were other powerful kings and queens in Europe

On the other side of the Atlantic...

It wasn't long before they started eyeing up South America too...

INCAS

*Does all this sound familiar??

Meanwhile, on the other side of the world...

55

AURANGZEB, Shah Jahan's son, was emperor for 50 years...
I had to imprison Dad for a while
... just a little mis-understanding!
heh heh
The empire grew even larger
AURANGZEB'S EMPIRE
ARABIAN SEA
But things weren't going well...
While Aurangzeb was away conquering, REBELLIONS sprang up
It's us again!
And us!
hnnnn
And us!!!
After Aurangzeb, his family argued about who should be the next emperor.
Me!
No, me!
WHACK
shriek
eek
urk
Gradually, the empire split up.
Eventually, a BRITISH TRADING COMPANY ended up controlling most of INDIA
What ho!
Any hunting round here, chaps?

Other Europeans were discovering much bigger things...

61

There was plenty to be afraid of at sea, not least...

Many of these pirates plundered the coast of America...

US SETTLERS

In 1607, Europeans founded their first COLONY in AMERICA.

Where's the nearest hostelry?

Funny headgear!

There was plenty of room for the new SETTLERS and NATIVE AMERICANS

The settlers would have starved to death

GROAN

It's not like Plymouth

... if the Native Americans hadn't helped them.

No... eat it!

Nice day

Not bad

There were lots of different groups of Native Americans but most of them got on with the settlers.

Until... in 1675 a chief called METACOM was peeved with the settlers of New Hampshire.

These settlers are stealing all my land

I've had enough of this!

Keep out!

snarl!

BIFF

WHACK

OW

eek

urk

So the settlers took their REVENGE...

ow

urk

uh

nng

aar

urk

Metacom was killed. His head ended up on a pole...where it stayed for 25 years. The Native Americans weren't quite so friendly after that...

In the south, settlers grew rich from crops like TOBACCO and SUGAR.

HACK HACK

ECK ECK

By 1770 the NEW WORLD relied on a TERRIBLE TRADE

COTTON SUGAR

AMERICA

EUROPE

Traded goods for SLAVES

Heh heh! Now you can work on my PLANTATION!

I'm not that keen actually

AFRICA

Different colonies of settlers got together and became the UNITED STATES of AMERICA.

ATLANTIC OCEAN

Later, they became an independent country (after a bit of a fight known as the WAR of AMERICAN INDEPENDENCE)

A few years later another revolution was brewing...

67

The Brits soon had a revolution
of their own...

For most of the 19th century, BRITAIN led the Industrial Revolution, and its empire got bigger and bigger...

While the Victorians were taking tea

...in AUSTRALIA the locals were receiving some unexpected visitors.

TRANSPORTATION to Australia as a punishment reached its peak around the 1830s.

There was CIVIL WAR in AMERICA when the southern states tried to leave the Union...

After four years of fighting, the northern states won. SLAVERY was abolished during the CIVIL WAR.

In CHINA there were OPIUM WARS...

In IRELAND there was a POTATO FAMINE...

Until 1854, foreigners weren't allowed into JAPAN and JAPANESE people weren't allowed out. Then...

There were lots of handy inventions in the 19th century,...

Time for another revolution...

83

Tracey Turner

Tracey Turner writes books for children
and adults about lots of different subjects,
including famous writers, rude words,
mysterious sliding rocks and, of course, the
entire history of the world. She lives in Bath
with Tom and their son, Toby. If she were
ever offered genetic modification, she thinks
wings might come in handy.

Sally Kindberg

Sally Kindberg is an illustrator and writer.
She once went to Elf School in Iceland, has
written a book about hair, and sailed on a
tall ship to Lisbon. She has one daughter,
Emerald, and lives in London with 67 robots.
She wishes she could swim like a fish.

www.sallykindberg.co.uk